THIS IS THE TRUTH

THIS IS THE TRUTH

Jennifer Kidney

Clare Songbirds
Publishing House

Clare Songbirds Publishing House Poetry Series
ISBN 978-1-957221-24-3
Clare Songbirds Publishing House
This is the Truth © 2025 Jennifer Kidney

Printed in the United States of America
FIRST EDITION

140 Cottage Street
Auburn, New York 13021
www.claresongbirdspub.com

For my sister, Pamela McCarter, who has her own version, and thanks to Cullen Whisenhunt for helping me get organized.

ACKNOWLEDGEMENTS

"St. Mary's River 1954," *The Seattle Review,* vol. II, no. 1 (Spring 1979)

"#MeToo," *Speak Your Mind* (anthology), Village Books Press, July 2019

"Iron Lung," "Mulberries and Roses," *PIECEWORK* (Winter 1988)

"Labor Day," from *Women Who Sleep with the Dogs*, Village Books Press, 2004

"Birthday Poem – 1958," from *Endangered Species*, renegade #2 (November 1984)

"Bean Years," *Ain't Gonna Be Treated This Way* (anthology), Village Books Press, July 2017

"Saying Grace," *Oklahoma Humanities* (Spring-Summer, 2023)

"A Photograph of My Lover at the Age of Four," *Kudzu* (Spring 1980)

"Packing My Bag," "Some Things I Lost," *Dragon Poet Review* (Spring 2018)

"Dream House," *Picking Up the Tempo*, no.2 (May 2007)

"Ghosts," *Renegade #5* (Summer 1985)

"American Literature," *Cross Timbers*, Vol. 11, no. 1 (Spring-Summer 2011)

"Driving to California," *Elegant Rage: A Poetic Tribute to Woody Guthrie* (anthology), Village Books Press, 2012

"Blue Moon in July," *Dragon Poet Review* (Summer 2016)

"Someone Should Be Named Carlos," *Dragon Poet Review* (Summer-Fall 2018)

"Vintage Years," *Oklahoma Humanities* (Fall/Winter 2019)

Table of Contents

This is the Truth

Sleeping With the Old People

1. Grandfather is dead
but Grandmother and Mother
and Father and I
still live to sleep
our lives away
sharing the same
king-sized bed
in the master bedroom.
Each night I lie
awake and listen
as Grandmother whimpers,
Father talks in his sleep
and Mother answers.
I watch their eyes move
beneath their eyelids.
Now Grandmother makes
a noise like a sewing machine,
Mother is playing a dirge
on the Wurlitzer of her dreams
and Father is fighting with Death:
"You son of a bitch" he snarls
in a voice distorted by dreaming.

2. It is ten years before my birth.
Grandmother weighs 200 pounds,
her hair is dyed black,
and she bakes cakes for extra money.
Mother is just a bride
and Father doesn't have a mustache.

Mother sings "Besame Mucho"
at the bowling banquet
where there is nothing much to eat
and Father works for the newspaper
and always wears his hat.

In the Paradise Palace
Mother and Father dance
to the music of big bands
which I hear from a distance
as if in a dream
and the dance drags on forever

and no one stops on a dime
for no one has a dime.

3. Something wakes me
as I lie in my crib
but I will be good—
I will not cry.

Awake I hear tires
crunching on gravel
and watch a rectangle of light
move around the room.

Outside I see the moon
close to the ground
and a mountain lion
leans in at the window.

Mother Chooses Names for Her Daughters

She was named Mildred
and although the youngest
she was the least favored child.
Her older sister Edna May
was blue-eyed and blonde
and deemed beautiful
and her brother, Albert,
was of course a boy
valued for his potential
to carry on the family name.
Mother's name determined
that she wore a Buster Brown bob
and scowled from childhood photographs
while Edna May sported ringlets
and beamed from the family album

Mother abhorred her name
which reminded her of mud
so before her daughters were born
she did research, unearthing
the poetry of possible appellations.
For my older sister she chose
Pamela, redolent of the sweet Greek honey
from which it was coined by a poet.
For me, she found Jennifer,
a modern Guinevere, meaning
"white wave"--a poem in itself.
She may have been aware
of the literary references--
Richardson's virtuous Pamela
and the adulterous Guinevere
of Arthurian legend--
but she gave us names she deemed
would be gifts of self esteem.

Hollyhocks
(Clarksburg, West Virginia, 1949)

At the brown and yellow bungalow on Terra Cotta Street
Mother fought the hollyhocks (she thought that they were weeds)
and lost. To me their ruffled pink and purple blooms
were like crepe-paper flowers that frill and festoon
birthday parties.

                         Our elegant next-door neighbors
took tea on their ragged lawn when afternoons were fair.
I ate their white bread and damson jam, but found them dull,
preferring milk and raisin bran at my orange-crate table.

Mother said the mountain folk crept out from under rocks
to come to town on Saturdays. I watched their children walk
past our house on the way to school. They would be barefoot
in warm weather; in snow, they wore black felt boots.

Mother complained the walls of our house were as thin
as cardboard. The house would moan and rock in the wind
of storms, while I stayed snug and dreamed oriental potentates
and aspiring angels in the blue flames of the asbestos grate.

When I was six years old, we moved away. Mother was glad
to leave the patchwork past behind, but I was sad
and wept, bereft, to lose the attic room where Mother kept
my baldheaded dolls and outgrown clothes in the cedar chest.

St Mary's River 1954

I would sit on the pier
until I felt it moving
out into the river.
I was so small
that I could only cling
to the post and listen
to the lop-lop of the water.

The gold-green water
would close around the chicken neck
tied to the string.
I would wait for the tug—
sometimes I thought
that it would pull me in—
pull up the string
until I felt the wet
and saw the tubular eye
and bright blue claw,
the shell of the body
the color of the river.

Hurricane Carol was named
for my silly sister who cried
at the scuttling of claws
against the iron boiling pot.
Mother had to throw them out
on the bank of the river
where I watched my father
cling to the post of the pier
as if he wished to pull it up
from the bottom.
He was so small
in the eye of the wind.

When Carol blew over
the sun came out clouded.
The river was muddied.
The spiderwebs glittered
through the cracks in the pier
where I sat close to the post
and sailed away.

Labor Day

The day before school begins,
the ocean laps at the front door
calling us out to play.
Venturing into the surf
we hold hands to avoid the undertow.
Tomorrow we return to our labors.

Today Father carves a sea captain
from driftwood, my sister traps
a box turtle, and I hunt
shells and sharks' teeth
along the beach. The afternoon
casts ominous shadows
and the ocean breeze chills us.

The mole comes out at dusk,
black and silky as summer night,
but we wear sweaters to our last supper
at the Crab House. The tablecloths
are newspapers with which we wrap
discarded shells and devil fingers;
our fingers sting from picking.

On this day summer ends.
We board the cottage windows,
lock the door, seal in the air
to store three seasons of mustiness.

Tomorrow we imagine everything is new,
sharp pencils, plaid dresses,
but we are only home again
and carry summer with us
like the hermit crab his borrowed house.

Dear Diary

It was pink with "My Diary"
embossed in gold on the cover.
It had a strap that fitted over
a metal loop to which
a heart-shaped lock attached.
I hid the tiny key,
but at the age of eight
what secrets had I to confide
to the wide-lined pages?
Not my own but what I observed
among my playmates more secure
in indulging their innate criminal natures.
Gerry cheated at marbles and hid
in the closet to evade his mother's
frequent tirades, and Carol pilfered
Ginny-doll clothes from Woolworth's.
I blithely believed in my right to privacy
and had sole possession of the key,
but I had a mother with a bobby pin
and a bent to satisfy her curiosity.
She unlocked the diary and exposed
my friends to their mothers' punishment
while I suffered from embarrassment.
I decided then that diaries are best
as a repository of fiction, or at least
some misleading embellishment
of secrets and the truth.

#MeToo

Sometimes memories
are like annoying pop-ups
in the brain's computer
needing tech support
to shut them up.

Today out of the gray
I remembered playing
with Marshall Windsor,
an older boy who lived
across the street.
I was wearing
a new sundress,
white with red polka dots,
rickrack trim, and buttons
down the front
that Mother had just made.

I was passing the time
before we went out to dinner
while my parents
finished their martinis.
Marshall and I
were playing tag,
chasing each other
around the trunk
of the enormous oak
in his front yard.

I was distracted
looking forward to dinner
at the Good Food Shoppe,
shrimp and crab
swimming in butter
and a salad topped
with an enticing
curl of carrot
that looked like a tongue.

My mouth was watering
when Mother called.
I began to run home

but Marshall grabbed
the back of my dress
and pulled so hard
that the buttons popped off.

I remember shock,
shame at being exposed
in my underwear,
and fear of not being allowed
to go out to dinner
although I was not to blame
for my ruined dress.

Why do I remember this now
so far from my eight-year-old self,
new homemade dresses,
childish anticipation
and ultimate disappointment?
I wish there were
keys to press
or an icon to click
to erase this mess
from my memory as easily
as I escaped my dress.

Iron Lung

We wore our green dresses
and merit badge sashes
to visit the girl in the iron lung.
We stood around her silver bed
in awe of her pallor as she lay in state.
She watched us in the mirror by her head,
sipped nectar through a straw,
asked and answered questions.

We made s'mores in her front yard
and told her what a pretty day it was
while all the time that foreign machine
groaned and heaved helping her breathe.
She was seventeen, had lain in her strange bed
for seven years, away from the seasons and the sun.
We wanted to know did she still grow?
Had she ever been in love?
When would the prince come to plant the kiss
that would stir her limbs to run?

Mulberries and Roses

Imitating Poe, Carol and I
wrote stories beneath the mulberry tree
while her brothers' shirts on the clothesline
flapped in the breeze. Like Huckleberry Finn
we envisioned our own funerals, our secret admirers
revealing themselves in their grief,
and promised never to send each other
roses for remembrance.
We were much rarer flowers.

We knew that silkworms fattened
on mulberry leaves, or was it the berries,
or were they the fat white berries?
Were those summer webs made of silk?
Carol climbed the tree to see.
The branches grew low and wide—an easy up.
But the fall was hard, flat on her back,
white as worm-web, breathless.
Had I taunted her to jump?

We'd gleefully steal
from her uncle's corner grocery,
getting away with nothing
as he winked knowingly:
Sugar Daddies, jars of olives
bulging from our pockets. We'd picnic
in the cemetery, the only park
in our part of town, and plan
our glamorous careers, romantic deaths.
We'd be Joan of Arc, Dale Evans,
Marilyn Monroe,
Florence Nightingale, Marie Curie,
Nancy Drew and more.

And all that happy time death stalked her
like a drugstore cowboy intent on rape
who won her at last
and the last time I saw Carol
she was fourteen years old,
perfectly porcelain beautiful
like a girl in a magazine,
dressed in her Easter suit,
propped on silken pillows
in a casket, surrounded by roses,
some with my name—both of us betrayed.

Birthday Poem –1958

In the white rented boot-skates
I push myself around the rink,
propelling myself from the rail,
seeking momentum. I long to sail
into the center and twirl the green
circle of my skirt, exposing knees
and underwear. I don't dare.
My sister's turtleneck makes me
Parisian or a beatnik, exotic
as a witch, eyelids magically
green, a pink smear on my lips.
There are boys who do not skate,
who slouch and watch and rock
to the loudspeaker beat of Clyde
McPhatter or the Monotones. At five
o'clock my magic boots turn into
bobby sox and saddle shoes.

Tonight my sister takes me to *Giselle*,
my first ballet. I weep and thrill
and when I close my eyes the ground still
whirls beneath me. I am Giselle,
or some other girl, less tragic,
Cinderella in gold lame, waltzing
with the Prince across a gleaming
floor, pirouetting on a stage.

Folding the Flag

Yesterday afternoon I saw
the principal of the elementary school
across the street hurriedly
lowering the American flag,
unceremoniously wadding it up,
and retreating indoors with the flag
bundled in her arms. In an era
when patriotism seems to take
sides, the flag seems to have
lost its meaning. As children
we were taught to respect
the flag, to pledge our allegiance
in grade school, to participate
in the flag-folding ritual
in Girl Scouts. We were never
to allow the flag to touch
the ground. While one of us
carefully lowered the banner
from its pole, two of us
caught the edges and a fourth
helped unfasten the rings.
It took all four of us to fold
the flag correctly, reverently,
one at each corner, as we folded
over and over until we had
a neat triangular packet,
stars facing skyward,
to await the next day's raising.
Now I see giant tattered flags
waving from the tops of bank buildings
day and night in all weather
or see them bedraggled and drooping
beside the garage of a suburban house
and never taken down.
We seem to have lost
respect for the flag
as well as each other,
a loss from which
we may never recover.

Dress Code

When I started first grade
a dress code was in place
which mostly seemed
to apply to girls.
Skirts were mandatory,
even on snowy days.
We tucked our snow pants
beneath our skirts,
removing them when we arrived
at school and stowing them
in the cloak room
(as it was then called,
as if we were attending Hogwarts,
not yet even imagined,
and wore our wizards' cloaks
en route to school).
I walked each day
to Henry Clay elementary
and frequently found myself
attracted by something shiny
or odd lying along the sidewalk.
Kneeling down to retrieve
a fascinating object—
bottlecap, rock, bubblegum charm—
I'd catch my heels
in the hem of my dress.
Blithely proceeding to school
muddied and bedraggled,
I was still wearing a skirt
and went unpunished.
Junior high and high school
were much the same,
although our hair, and later,
make-up, passed without comment.
While our hair-dos got higher
and we discovered eye-liner,
our skirts gradually grew shorter.
But at last one day in May
we celebrated "Bermuda Day"
when we were allowed to swap
our skirts for bermuda shorts,
preferably a muted madras plaid
paired with a pastel button-down shirt,
a new preppy dress code
we had fashioned for ourselves.

Drug Store Cowboys

My father called the men
who frequented Flax's Deli and Bar
"drug store cowboys."
This made sense to me.
I passed that establishment
on my way to Drug Fair
to consider swiping
a Tangee lipstick
or to Lee Market to buy
some essential for dinner.
I often encountered
a handsome black man
lingering outside the door
who wore pearl snap
cowboy shirts with a bandanna
jauntily tied at his throat
but who'd proudly announce
to any passers-by
"I'm a full-blooded Nava-Joe."
I wasn't old enough to enter
the dimly lit bar, but knew
my grandpa had been inside
for a sip of forbidden whiskey
that Grandma wouldn't allow.
Mother and Grandma knew
Flax's was a "den of iniquity"
from which predatory young men,
lounge lizards and GI's in civvies,
would spill out to the sidewalk
to smoke cigarettes and wolf whistle
as I hurried by in fear
of attack from those drug store
cowboys and even Indians!

Killing Spiders

It was my father
who told me
that killing a spider
would make it rain.
Later I discovered
Huck Finn and Tom Sawyer
decimating spiders to spoil
the Sunday School picnic.
I killed two spiders today,
one dangling from the towel
I'd grabbed to dry my face,
another creeping across
the kitchen floor.
Good, I thought.
We need rain.
And rain did fall
everywhere but here.
There was a promising
gust of wind,
thunder and lightning,
but not a drop
sizzling on the flagstones
or drenching the parched plants
wilting in the flower beds.
Perhaps it's better
to be a Buddhist,
to coax an arachnid
onto my palm and gently
replace it outdoors.

When Scottie Lanahan Visited

My father considered himself
a newspaper man
although he was neither
editor nor reporter.
He was an artist,
the lay-out man and illustrator,
inserting a drawing
in the absence of a photograph,
designing advertisements
and selecting the fonts
for the typesetters
and proofing the plates
of every page
reading backwards
before the Daily Sun
went to press.

My father and his editor,
who had an illustrious past
in bigger towns than ours,
were fast friends.
When Scottie Lanahan
dropped in one day
to reminisce, my father,
impressed, suggested
cocktails at our house,
my mother dragooned
as hostess, passing out
fancy hors d'oeuvres—
smoked oysters and shrimp
and artichoke hearts
impaled on frilled toothpicks—
while my father mixed the drinks.

Scottie and the editor
exchanged anecdotes
of colleagues past and present,
scandalous and hilarious,
their repartee peppered
with curse words
while my father laughed

and Mother's smile
was tightly compressed.

I was beguiled by Scottie's
long hair, almost to her shoulders,
her jaunty beret, her crisp white shirt
and length of lustrous pearls,
her tight tweed skirt
and slender ankles crossed,
her plain black pumps
slightly dusty and scuffed.

After our guests departed,
my carefully coifed mother remarked,
Did you see her hair,
just hanging down
as if she were ready for bed?
And she wasn't wearing stockings!
This detail my mother found shocking.

But I'll always remember
how graceful Scottie seemed,
the embodiment of glamorous.
I sensed somehow she was famous
but had no idea who she was,
a journalist herself
and the child of a renowned novelist,
as I learned years later,
and my mother was simply jealous.

Misconceptions

Eighth grade was nearing its end—my birthday had passed and Easter was on the horizon. Because my mother was staying at my grandparents' house recovering from a serious operation to remove a part of her lung, my father and I were "baching" it. We did our best to replicate her nightly dinners—protein, vegetable, starch— although I'm sure that Kraft Macaroni and Cheese and Noodles Romanoff had a heavy rotation. Mother was so ill that I wasn't even allowed to visit her, and of course she had been unable to make my annual birthday-Easter dress. My father was no help in such matters, so I took my birthday money—probably less than $20—and walked to Sears-Roebuck in Clarendon to buy a suitable dress. Outside the curtained dressing rooms was an enigmatic sign: Do Not Try On Bathing Suits During Monthly. "Monthly what?" I puzzled. I decided it must mean "monthly sale" when too many people would want to try on bathing suits for the dressing rooms to accommodate them.

Years later, while reminiscing about that strange time without Mother, my aunt Edna confided that the real reason I was not allowed to see Mother was that she was going through withdrawal from the copious amounts of morphine administered to her in the hospital. "You wouldn't have known her—she was completely out of her mind, simply raving mad," exclaimed Aunt Edna. Also years later, but without any input from my elders, I realized that "monthly" in the mysterious Sears sign referred to one's "period" —a euphemism that we still use for menstruation—or "the curse," as my mother called it. This revelation was almost more shocking than the one about my mother's temporary insanity. The Sears sign seemed to be an invasion of bathing suit shoppers' most intimate privacy, but then I wondered why such signs are no longer posted or deemed necessary.

Life is full of mysteries and poses many questions that might best be left unanswered. As for the dress I bought—a fully-lined lavender linen short-sleeved shift—I wore it only once to church on Easter Sunday, after which it was sweat-stained and wrinkled beyond resurrection.

February Fourteenth

Snow was rare in Tidewater. It fell miraculously
one year when Valentine's Day fell on a Sunday.
It was Teddy's birthday. I drew teddy bears to show
that I loved him. When I was sixteen there was snow
again and mysterious footprints leading to the mailbox
where I found a poem signed by a car: Hot Rod Dodge.
Years later, Teddy wrecked his Ferrari on a wild winding
Italian road. I received anonymous early spring
flowers: daffodils, tiny pink roses, baby's breath.
I've had no valentines for fourteen years,
fourteen lines of a sonnet, which I remember,
for tradition says sonnets are love poems; love's day,
February fourteenth. Today. The snow melts away;
the world is white with fog; I think of death.

21

Archive.org
Penman – Fall 1963

When I was seventeen, I wrote maudlin
yet skillful sonnets while simultaneously
promoting "vers libre" as the perfect vessel
for expressing adolescent angst.
All of this is documented on-line,
I discovered by chance while "googling" myself.
I was surprised at the sonnets, although I remember
my broken heart that I disguised with cynicism.
I remember the assassination of the President
that wrapped a pall around every human activity.
I remember playing hookie to ride the bus downtown
where monuments of government and diplomacy loomed
above the sticky diesel popcorn smell of the pavement.
My best friend had taken another bus
to Port Authority and New York City,
running away from home, but I had never thought
to include any of my real life in a poem.

Why I Hate Opera

My mother was a master
delegator of tasks.
On Saturday mornings
when she worked at the bank
she'd leave a jar
filled with housekeeping chores
written on slips of paper
for my father and me to perform
before she came home
at noon. After grocery shopping
and lunch, she'd ensconce
herself in her armchair,
put her feet up,
and turn on the radio at 2 p.m.
while I was stationed
at the ironing board
to smooth the week's washing
rolled into damp tubes
snugged in the laundry basket
awaiting the thunk of the iron
and the rising steam
as I chased the wrinkles away.
While Mother sipped her postprandial beer
and listened to the mellow voice
of Milton Cross announcing
the soaring arias and choruses sung
in Italian or German
by the Metropolitan Opera
far away in New York City
I was sweating through
my father's dress shirts,
napkins, and bed sheets,
a captive audience for music
I did not appreciate.
Now opera reminds me of servitude
worse than that of Aida
and I don't like ironing either.

Bean Years

After my sister left home
and my father lost his job
at the end of every week
my mother made a pot of beans
navy beans (which, oddly, were white)
left to soak on the stove on Friday night
then simmered all of Saturday
with a ham bone begged from the butcher.
Saturday night we'd eat a watery soup
with chunks of cornbread. On Sunday
it would be repurposed with cabbage.
On Monday, celery, carrots, and potatoes were added.
My mother was a frustrated gourmet chef
who dreamed of Shrimp Creole and Beef Stroganoff
but those meals were in the future.
To this day I remember those white beans
with the occasional pink sprout curling out
from within one. Even with the fancy French name,
Cassoulet, I vow never to eat those beans again.

Saying Grace

Recipes might be
poems or prayers,
incantations
of ingredients,
litanies of steps
to gain our daily bread.
Mix, add, stir, spread,
bake and pray
that the cake will rise
in the warm dark
of the preheated oven.
Dice the trinity,
onion, bell pepper, celery;
saute, sprinkle in the flour
and paddle the roux
until it's gilded and thickened.
Add tomatoes, okra, chicken
and simmer, simmer
until it's time to dive
into the holy mumbo-jumbo
of Creole gumbo.
We reverently request
that this meal may be blessed
as we have faithfully
followed the recipe.

My Ex-Husband's Italian Family on his Mother's Side

I learned much from those Italian aunts
and uncles and cousins. I learned
that pizza is just pie, although it wasn't
my idea of pie, and included spinach pie,
a loaf of chewy Italian bread
with a molten middle of spinach
and ricotta, a prized dish for Sunday brunch.
The aunts and cousins vied
in a friendly way to concoct the darkest,
richest Sunday sauce. They began with the herbs—
Mario Batali would have scoffed
at their technique—sauteed in pungent olive oil
with garlic and onions, and then they'd add the meat.
Did you know that tomatoes are American
in origin? And pasta's roots are in China.
Without the exploits of my in-laws'
adventurous countrymen, there'd be no
spaghetti sauce, there'd be no spaghetti—
such are the twists of tradition.

The aunts and uncles were all
first generation immigrants—
Luigi, Paolo, Alberto, Maria,
Firenza, Costanza, Giannetta—
but quickly assumed American identities—
Uncle Lou, Uncle Paul, Uncle Al,
Aunt Mary, Aunt Florence, Aunt Connie,
Aunt Jeanette. The second generation
male cousins formed a doo-wop band
in the early sixties while their female counterparts
attended nursing school or became secretaries,
but all were connoisseurs of mysterious sauces
and spinach pie, not to mention cannoli,
the favored kind with dark chocolate bits
rather than candied fruit.

They disapproved of me, of course.
I'd eschewed the lengthy Catholic wedding

followed by the six-course celebratory meal,
although I'd eaten my way through a few of those,
but my husband was only half theirs,
carrying on their dark eyes and curly hair.
And to this day, I can make
eggplant caponata and Sunday sauce
with the best of them.

Independence Day

Brown and blond, he slips
his jeans and blue shirted
shoulders into the red seat
of the low yellow car.
It bucks away in the direction
of sunset: pink clouds
on a deepening blue sky.

I am left with my independence
and a red brick house
with only one story
on a rise from which to see
the sun rise and set
and fireworks: spider mums
on a navy blue kimono.

As the sky turns cobalt
I write my name
beneath the stars with a sparkler
and watch its glowing letters
vanish in the dark.

A Photograph of My Lover at the Age of Four

Your chubby arms are lifted
to the sky, reflected in your eyes,
and your smile is full of teeth
and glee; you seem to see
something too wonderful for words
that curdles you to laughter
like your mother's tickle games
or a teddy bear that talks.

I see you then and now
with thirty years' perspective.
Now you are tall, so you stoop;
your eyes are blue like steel
with a green glint at their centers;
but when you laugh, you're helpless
as a boy dissolved at his mother's ambush.
I am still robbing the cradle.

The Last Compliment

We were never meant
to be together
but were drawn
to one another
like moths to light.
You thought I was a dancer.
I thought you were a holy man,
a gentle saint
with a wild streak,
the pistol under the driver's seat,
the bottle of fortified wine
in the glove box.
I gave you poems
in exchange for paintings
at our rare meetings.
The last time we met
we reached to embrace
but refrained. The last
words you said to me:
"You've held up pretty well."
Not much of a compliment,
but I'll forever treasure it.
Now that you're gone,
no other can match it.

Purple Cauliflowers

In Memory of Someone I Loved

1.

He has a lust for life and nature
undampened by cancer, pain, and loss
that inspires the purest love.
Bad hair or no hair or "gimme" cap,
a gap-toothed grin, coveralls
or overalls hanging on a lanky frame,
he's a beautiful man trampling
through the swampy underbrush
to flush out a rare bird.

2.

After catfish and a drive through the refuge
to gape at prothonotary warblers and indigo buntings,
little blue herons and variegated fritillaries
floating down like out of season autumn leaves,
he says, "Let's drive to my place
to see my purple cauliflowers."
I've never heard of such a thing
but don't question him out of respect.

His garden is much like mine,
fringed with woody salvia and dotted
with bright annuals in clay pots,
and towering over all
are the purple coneflowers.
I'm glad I held my tongue.

3.

A friend calls
to tell me of his death.
I thought he'd be
like the Oklahoma wind,
never out of breath.
Now all his energy
and anger, too,
I realize now,
is extinguished
and he's at last at rest.

4.

Everything in the yard
reminds me of him.
The deciduous holly
he promised me
is now loaded with berries.
"You need more trees,"
he said. "If you'd deadhead
the spirea, it'll keep blooming."
That task I found too daunting.
And, of course, there are the echinaceas,
purple coneflowers
reseeding themselves
to come back again
year after year,
outlasting us all.

5.

Months later
I still expect him to call.
"How you Jen?"
he'd say,
to which I'd respond
"I beg your pardon?"
What an odd question.
What does it mean?
"I don't understand you."
Perhaps that was the problem
all along.

Un-Sonnet

The last man I loved is dead
so of course my head is filled
with conversations I wish I'd had--
not terms of endearment
or confessions of commitment
deeply felt but never fully expressed;
instead I need arguments settled,
explanations clarified, all on my side,
but never his. He was a garrulous old man
who never really listened,
and now that he's dead
I'll be forever misunderstood.
There'll be no heavenly reconciliation,
but only this limbo of frustration,
words unspoken, language as lost
as an unimagineable paradise.

Packing My Bag

I'm vacationing in Mexico
with a girlfriend who's easily seduced
by a bad poet, an ex-pat Gringo
reciting a villanelle. His affected intonations
so irritate the bartender and waiters
that they begin to shoot
all of the ugly Americans,
including my lover, although I know
he's already dead, downed back home
by a sheriff's deputy intimidated
by that gentle man wielding a machete.
My dream gives us a second chance.
I fold his frail body into my suitcase.
When we arrive at the airport, I realize
I can't carry him through security,
so I open my bag to find him alive
and healed and heading off to buy
his ticket home, and I acknowledge
he is part of my baggage
that I will always carry with me.

Ghosts
in memory of Roxy Gordon

I see your haunted hooded eyes
across the restaurant table.
One friend has died, another
come back from the dead.
And I am tormented
by yet another pair of eyes
that stare me out of sleep
and reason. Haunted and hung over,
we are startled by a napkin
caught in the draft of the fan.
"Look, a ghost," exclaims
your four-year-old.
We acknowledge his wisdom.

When we were children, we were frightened
by our ghosts because we hadn't learned
to recognize them. Our mothers counseled us:
"It's only thunder, just the wind,
the dark, a bad dream."

Then we sought them out for the thrill,
pitching a tent in the back yard,
daring them to make a midnight visitation.

Finally we invented them,
the man in the hat who offered us
sweets, a ride to the grocery store,
the strange old lady down the street
who ate little children who ran away from home.

Now our ghosts are everywhere.
Even the daylight is haunted. Beware
of gifts, letters, telephone calls at two a.m.,
the corners you turn, your dreams.

I believe in ghosts; I always have.
I respect your ghosts.
You respect mine.

Dream House

The house of my dreams
is a large pink Victorian
with turrets and curlicues,
gingerbread trim and fan lights,
and many tall windows
with wavy glass
catching distorted reflections
like fun-house mirrors.
The house looks like a wedding cake
and first appeared
after my abortion.
Mother and Grandma were there
bustling about the kitchen
discussing nutrition.
They are often inside
the house, as is my father.

Sometimes the house sits
on an island
or I discover deep crevasses
have appeared in the lawn
overnight. Once the interior
was transformed into an arena,
the site of a huge rock concert,
and Bob Dylan stood
at the foot of the winding stair
and sang his new song.
Mother and Grandma
were smoking dope
and I couldn't remember
the words when I awoke.

Other times the floors
fall away or the walls
move to reveal secret rooms.
Once I discovered a magic shop
behind the bedroom. Masks
covered the walls and wands,
cards, crystal balls, and potions
sat in glass cases. Beyond this
was the biergarten-delicatessen,

dark beer and sausages
and chocolate cake being consumed
by bland overweight strangers
laughing loudly. I felt
put upon and invaded.

Lately, I've discovered
a fully furnished attic
up a narrow stairway
behind a panel in the hall.
Many-paned windows
wrap the room which contains
a tiny antique bed
covered with a patchwork quilt
and a kind of altar
on which stands a lovely
kimono-clad porcelain doll,
the kind I longed to possess
when I was a child,
and I realize
all this
has always been mine.

Some Things I Lost

There was that turquoise earring
that somehow got ejected
from my purse as I rummaged
for my credit card so I could
do self-check-in at 4 a.m.
at Will Rogers Airport.
I didn't notice it was missing
until much later while unpacking
in a D.C. hotel room.
My friend Judy later told me
that if you lose a piece of turquoise
it was never meant to be yours.
I suppose that's true
of everything you lose.

Then there are the socks.
I live alone except for a few cats
and a dog, but I keep losing socks.
Sometimes I find them
wadded up inside a neatly folded
pair of jeans, and sometimes a cat
will suddenly appear dragging a sock
like prey from the secret place
where she had hidden it.

And lovers? All lost, although
of most, I must say
"Good riddance."
Yet they, too, often reappear
unbidden in my dreams.

And there are the inevitable losses
that come with growing older,
loved ones who can never be found again
unless there really is a heaven.
I imagine a place where my family and friends
are gathered, wearing mismatched odd socks
and earrings, awaiting my arrival
to make things even again.

Driving to California
1974

The cowboy boots in the Amarillo sign
were aptly yellow. "Fastest Route
to the Coast" the sign proclaimed.
Each time I drove to the city,
I longed to follow Route 66
to the sea. In Arizona I'd stop
at every trading post getting
cheated for treasures: bracelets of tin
and turquoise, blue as the sky
or the thin places on the thighs of my jeans.
I'd gawk at giant rattlers in cages
at roadside snake farms and look forward
to rock museums, dream movies
and open my eyes on their scenes
all around me: saguaro cactus
and mountains in the distance.
In the purple desert
west of Flagstaff, Indian ponies
would munch the sparse grasses
and pose for my photographs. At last
where the wintry Pacific boils
along the beach, a hundred times
my heart would fall from the brink
of the cliff: the sun sets there.
Through orange and olive groves,
promised land of milk and honey,
I'd pursue the undulation of the road
to San Francisco where narrow pink
buildings, exuberant, insane, cling
to a precarious existence on the edge of things.
I'd take the "loneliest road" back home,
bringing along turquoise, beach stones,
sequoia nubs, a sack of dirty clothes.
There would still be snow
from Wolf Creek Pass
on the underside of the car.
It would melt and become absorbed
in the gray cement of the garage floor.

American Literature

It is Saturday afternoon.
I cannot read *Huckleberry Finn*
for the seventh time when now
I stop at every second word,
make notes in red ink in two places:
the margin and this sheet of
recycled wide-ruled three-ring
loose-leaf notebook paper.

I hunger for food not to be found
in the refrigerator which hums
while I turn on the radio.
The dog is restless, too.
He whines and skulks and watches
my every move. No one will visit,
for these afternoons become
Saturday nights which are all
prearranged. The phone won't ring.

The snow ceases to melt as the sun
sets. I turn the TV on without the sound
and watch a basketball rebound.
The drapes are drawn. Last night's dancing
blue and gold fire is cold chalk-like
ashes on the hearth. The snow turns
to ashes in the twilight. The streetlight
winks in the space where the drapes part.

The dog falls asleep, resigned.
I take up my book and float
down the fog-bound Mississippi
away from freedom again.

Smoking Window
1980

Flying home, into winter,
into the family room where my father
has come from the hospital to die,
my preferred seat is a "smoking window."
The phrase evokes a house ablaze
on a morning so cold that words are visible
as cartoon balloons and stars have formed
on the windshield. I fly above the weather,
gazing down at a flying carpet of clouds
capable of all the fairytale imagery
of childhood. When the NO SMOKING sign
goes off, I light a cigarette.

My father is dying of Christmas,
of cancer. I order a Bloody Mary
from the ageing stewardess. I look out
at angel hair, snow, Santa Claus's
white curly beard. I look forward
to a Christmas of disappointment,
the dining room disputes, the kitchen bitches
in the bosom of my family.

But nothing can happen to me here
suspended, unmoved in mid-air.
Nothing can happen as we descend
through clouds, as the Appalachians,
firred and iced, rise to meet us.
Nothing can happen except the crash and blaze,
the windows smoking, exploding, melting the snow.

Just My Imagination

The greatest insult
Mother could inflict
was when she said,
"You have no imagination."
That was her response
to any skepticism expressed
at her latest drastic narrative:
her Wurlitzer organ was bugged,
she insisted, and her original songs
pilfered by the likes
of Englebert Humberdinck
and Vicki Carr, or the janitor
from the bank mysteriously appeared
on the upper tier of Kann's parking garage
hurling stones at shoppers below.
These stories could not be true,
we thought, but now I think
that Mother knew this to be so,
that they were stories
that required us to use
our imagination
to unwind their meaning.
At other times
Mother accused me of having
too much imagination.
My childhood was filled
with hallucinations:
fairies dancing around
the stump of a tree
I passed en route to school,
the gigantic rabbit
that loomed over my bed
one Easter morning,
and my imaginary friends—
constant companions
on whom I blamed
my childish transgressions,
crayon scribbles on the wall,
invisible slits in the ugly curtains,
all wrought behind my back,

I claimed. I guess
Mother and I were alike,
both of us needing that core
of magic in imagination
that made us the heroines
of our own stories.

Lessons

The last time
I saw my mother alive
in her hospital bed
I noticed how pretty she was
without her make-up--
her silky lashes
and aquamarine eyes--
while she eyed me
critically. "Why
do you wear your hair
like that?" It was long
and straight and I explained
my hair was fine
and too fragile
for a permanent wave,
too thin to be cut short.
"It's awful," she said.
And then she spied
the wide belt
cinching my tunic.
"Some belt," she commented
derisively.
I forgive her
because I remember
the storybook lady
who read to me
so expressively
tales about ingenuity
and bravery and pointed me
gently to lessons I've borne
through all of my years.

This is the Truth

From a recording left to me by my mother.

The tape recording begins
with Mother at her Wurlitzer,
the syncopated rhythm turned on,
pounding out an unrecognizable tune
to which Fritz the dachshund sings along.
Then the reminiscences begin.
Mother and her older sister, Aunt Eddie,
sound a trifle tipsy, their usual precise
enunciation blurred, their voices husky
from whiskey. Now both widowed,
they find themselves alone together.
Aunt Eddie, the elder by six years,
is about to reveal a family secret.
The narrative is somewhat disjointed,
interrupted by sips of Manhattans
and drags on Virginia Slims
and my mother's exclamations.

The revelation opens mildly.
"I read in the paper where a third cousin died,"
Aunt Eddie says, smothering a laugh.
"She was the organist at the Methodist Church.
She was only sixty-five when she died."
At this, Aunt Eddie laughs out loud.
"What was her name?" asks Mother.
"Miriam Jeffers." Mother remembers
the handsome brothers, one of whom
escorted her to Robin Hood Dell
when she was twelve. "There were five boys
and one girl, and Miriam never married."
Aunt Eddie's tone conveys an odd mix
of pity and scorn. She follows with a litany
of the brothers' feats, one the president of a bank,
another an architect. "The Jeffers
were 'be-yoo-ti-ful' people. Nobody smoked,
nobody drank, nobody ever did a damn thing.
They were just 'be-yoo-ti-ful,'
they really were." The ice cubes clink
in Aunt Eddie's glass. Mother interjects
that Aunt Ceil took her to the beauty parlor

45

for her first permanent wave that same summer
when she visited the beautiful Jeffers cousins.

"I want you to know, Millie," Aunt Eddie continues,
"Our grandfather Brown had ten children.
This is the truth. What I'm telling you
is the truth. One rainy day, I said,
'Mom, tell me. If you die, we won't know
where we came from.' And she told me
about her mother Ellen who married
the black sheep of a prominent family.
He was a head shorter than Ellen,
but he was the most handsome man
you ever saw. He didn't have the time of day
for us grandkids, but he'd pay us a nickel
for every potato bug we plucked from his plants.
But he was terrible, he was really terrible.
When Ellen died, Mom and her sisters
went to the house and took the things they wanted.
This is the truth. The next day
Grandpa called and said they must bring
everything back, they didn't deserve anything.
Two weeks later, he married his mistress."
"My grandfather had a mistress?" Mother shrieks.
"He'd had a mistress for fifteen years.
Grandpa was a traveling salesman,
and his mistress owned a hotel."
The dog begins to bark
as the women's voices rise.
"Is this the truth?" asks Mother.
"I'm telling you the truth."

"In the meantime—this is the truth, Millie
—he called Mom and said he was bringing
the new wife to dinner. You would have thought
that the Queen of England was coming.
Mom went all out even though she didn't approve.
And I remember it, Millie. I was about seven
and you were just a baby. She was a bleached blonde,
but very attractive, a head taller than Grandpa.
Well, she was really a whore. I don't know
how Mom did it. I would have just died.
And there were no drinks in those days,
but Mom made the best of it. And now I think

46

how terrible that must have been for Mom."
"Yes, Mom endured many terrible things,"
Mother responds. "Mom was something else."
"Well, I think I'm boring you,"
Aunt Eddie says with finality,
and the tape abruptly ends.

I turn off the player, eject the tape, and wonder
how Mother could possibly have been bored
by such a titillating tale, and why she didn't ask
for more details. Then I think back
to the beginning of the story
into which Mother was able to insert
her twelve-year-old self.
Aunt Eddie was already married then,
living in Philadelphia, and couldn't share
that memory, but Aunt Eddie's own recollection
of the family scandal
left Mother precariously dangling
from her limb on the family tree.
<u>This</u> is the truth.

This is the End

Turn The Page

The idea of a new year
is merely a metaphor.
A fresh page on which
a new story can begin
is simply human artifice,
a desperate attempt to control
inexorable nature
that waxes and wanes
as it must and resists
our efforts to shape it.
Imagine life without a calendar,
how immense the import
of sunrise and sunset,
the phases of the moon,
the poise of stars
that could still be seen
as they wheeled minutely
from place to place
in immeasurable space.
Everything would seem slower.
The movie trope
of days and months
flying from the calendar
not yet envisioned,
counting down
to the drop of a ball
inconceivable,
just unmeasured
yet rhythmic movement
through light and dark,
heat and cold,
plenty and scarcity.
But the impulse to measure,
to count, to look forward
and backward, was inevitable.
Our ancestors counted the moons,
mapped the movement of planets,
gave names to everything
and invented the calendar
by which life's motion
is imprisoned,
and so we turn the page.

Tabula Rasa

The white sky
of this January morning
is a blank page
on which to write
the day's story,
a chance to translate
random scratches
of stark limbs
and erratic flights
of dark birds
into something precise
and meaning filled,
like a blind oracle
who sees the future
by counting wingbeats
of hawks or geese.
My own insight
seems muddled and dim,
so instead I simply
pencil a list
to shape this day
into what I wish.

Ode to Mary Oliver

A friend said to me
that my poems reminded her
of Mary Oliver
so of course I had to buy
a book, the one with the most
new and selected
more bang for the buck
since I have always been poor
in terms of money
but I prefer my books of poetry
to be on my own shelves
rather than borrowed
from a library.

Black bears
were everywhere
and the lingering scent
of skunk in moist morning air
and birds here and there
as well as the ghost of Tecumseh
and the mindless decimation
of the buffalo
but I didn't find myself
except perhaps for a longing
to live close to fields and woods
where there'd be no need
to tend a garden and pull weeds.

My own yard abounds in birds
but rarely an owl or a heron
except for a glimpse in flight
but my poems might decipher
the haunting song of a bird
I have yet to see
or discern the meaning
of a deep winter slumber
where bears might stumble
into my dreams
but nevertheless I guess
I'll accept what I suppose
was a compliment.

Lightning Didn't Strike
a publisher's assessment of my manuscript

The half-dead redbud
in the front yard
still stands.
I want to paint it,
not to make a painting of it,
but to lacquer its trunk
and limbs with layers
of glossy enamel,
black at the base,
then mossy green
to the crooks of its arms
and hot pink fingers
mimicking spring bloom.
The critic, however,
suggests I'd be better off
chopping it down to the ground.

Half Remembered

Flags at half staff
on a windy winter day.
I have to stop and think
who died? What disaster
has befallen now?
There are too many
to remember
and too few noted
with any kind of tribute.
Who warrants this symbolic
condolence? No overdosed
musician, no victims
of an ubiquitous
school or shopping mall
shooting spree. Probably
some politician past
his sell-by date
now lying in state
on the way to the grave.

Remember to Forget

Sometimes I can't remember
what it was I couldn't remember
when I was talking with my neighbor,
my sister, myself. My recollection
is vague, but it was probably a name.
I always remember my sister's name
although she sometimes calls me
by her daughter's or granddaughter's name.
I call my dog by the cat's name
and vice versa, but they both respond
to the calling tone of voice.
Mnemonic devices and rote
are no use—perhaps I should try
Prevagen—but the problem
is ubiquitous and obvious,
recurrent and redundant.
What's the word for something
like that? Truism, perhaps?
I know it starts with a T.
I sift through the files
of my little gray cells
until I find this tautology:
I can't remember what I forgot.

No Memories Today

Facebook tells me I have
"No Memories Today,"
which is, of course,
nonsense. I have
memories every day.
My memories are a map
of what makes me "Me"
although if I'm honest
with myself, the ones
that crop up suddenly
or frequently recur
are more like acid reflux
than a reminiscent flavor
or evocative aroma.
Maybe I'd be better off
without them, those nagging
reminders of missteps
and impediments
in my autobiography.

In Greek mythology,
Mnemosyne,
the goddess of memory,
is the mother of the muses.
If I had no memories,
would Erato elude me
and my poems be unwritten?

And if we truly had
"No Memories Today"
would we still be ourselves?
I think of the blank stares
and vague smiles gracing
the faces of residents
in the nursing home,
dulled vision searching
for some glimmer of recollection.
Their memories are lost
to themselves and saved only
if once shared with others
who may remember for them
and for posterity so that
their memories may be more
than merely everyday.

The Santa Fe Look

I'm at a glitzy party
dressed up as I'll ever be
but nothing too shiny
or revealing—hair in a chignon,
nickel silver and beadwork earrings,
black top, long print skirt,
and sandals. Three guests,
wine glasses in hand,
approach, looking me
up and down, nodding,
saying, "Yes, we're really
into it." Into what?, I ask.
"The Santa Fe look."
I'm at a loss and explain
that my earrings are actually
Kiowa, my skirt a Carol Little,
but they've lost interest
and wander off to get more wine.

I'm in the check-out line
at Target on a winter afternoon
clad in my rust-colored coat,
booted and wearing jeans,
my hair in braids
when the woman behind me
says she really likes my coat,
my hair. "You look
like you're from Santa Fe."
With some hesitation,
I say thank you, guessing
this may be a compliment

I never much liked Santa Fe,
although it's beautiful,
filled with art, intriguing
artifacts, Spanish architecture,
flamenco dancing, and opera.
I have always felt alien there,
sensed a coolness in the air
that had nothing to do
with the weather. Perhaps
the Santa Fe look is like
R.C. Gorman's chili pepper women
on the painful verge of evolving
but not yet one or the other.
But no—that would be the Taos look!

New Shoes

In my seventies
the new shoes
that bring me joy
are not pretty
fire-hydrant red
pointy-toed pumps
with teetering
stiletto heels
but down to earth
dirt-brown sandals
with velcro closures
and excellent
arch support
that do not pinch
my toes or chafe
the backs of my ankles.
I'm far beyond
the need for flattery
and simply happy
to be able to keep
my feet on the ground.

Silver Tuesday

Tuesday is senior discount day
at Ross Dress for Less
and I'm on the hunt
for skinny jeans and a fetching top
that will make me look
too young for the discount.
When I pull into the parking lot
my Toyota Corolla abuts
the pick-up truck
of two young men engaged
in a heated argument,
but when I step out of the car
their eyes turn my way
and I'm surprised by wolf whistles
and "Hey, pretty mama!"
Thirty years ago
I would have been outraged
by this mindless objectification
of my sexuality, but today
I just smile to myself and sashay
into the store thinking
"Mama? Hah! I'm old enough
to be your Grandma!"
When I recount this event
at Wednesday's Social Security lunch
a not so friendly friend suggests
that it's my dyed red hair.
Well, maybe, but frankly,
I don't care!

Losing Your Marbles

Cat's Eye marbles
the prize at the bottom
of the cereal box,
swirled glass marbles
wisely crafted from shards
of McCoy pottery,
the gift of black and white
marbles, like the markers
from a set of Chinese checkers,
from the daughter of my neighbor
who felt I needed them,
the hand-made marble
with red eyes and green brows
bestowed by a long-ago boyfriend--
I still treasure all of them,
nestled in boxes
and the bases of vases,
and remember complex games,
the point of which
was to capture and keep
your opponent's marbles
until he lost all of his.

Cataracts

A cataract is a towering
fall of water descending
to a swirling stream
at the base of a mountain,
something impressive, majestic,
as seen in *National Geographic*.
Less commonly, a cataract
is a sudden downpour,
a gully-washer, as some might say,
that resembles a waterfall
arcing from the roof's eaves.
A cataract is a cloud on the lens
of an eye, caused by too much sun,
perhaps, that can afflict
even dogs, not only humans.
There was a cat in my cataract
and the tree of life that blocked
my vision of my real cats
and the trees in the yard.
These cataracts may be
signs of aging, of being
too long in the light
of the world, a hint from nature
that it's time to look inward
and take a final inventory.
But modern ophthalmology
relieves me of that responsibility.
When I open my eyes now
it seems as if someone
has washed the windows.

You Deserve a Break Today

Weight and blood pressure checked,
I'm waiting for the doctor
to enter the exam room.
To pass the time, I gaze
out the window at roofers
who resemble tiny action figures
sprawled here and there along
the peaks of an apartment complex
across the street. Parts of the roof
are shrouded in white particle board
making it appear like
a snow-covered mountain range
from my vantage in this bleak cubicle
where the air-conditioning mimics
wintry air but outside I know
it's in the nineties and those nimble roofers
are sweating as they drag shingles
to cover that white expanse
gleaming in the distance.
I turn to the book I've brought
where the characters are taking
sleigh rides or huddled before a fireplace
sipping hot chocolate.The pages
are diminishing as I near the end
but I don't want to finish, not yet,
not here. Where is the doctor?
I've had enough of waiting
and escape my cell to tell
the receptionist I'm leaving,
but there's no escape. A nurse
ushers me back, reassuring me
the doctor will soon appear.
He does, asks and answers
a few questions, and departs,
as do I, but on my way out
I'm handed an envelope
with a consolation prize--
a ten dollar gift card
to McDonald's. Apparently
I deserve a break today!

Physical Therapy

In the saltwater pool
of the physical therapy center
they are buoyant.
Their legs float out
to the back or the side
as they grasp the bar.
Unlike me, they have no fear
of the deep end. But when
their sessions are over,
their wheelchairs are rolled
to the edge of the pool
and the attendants
hand them towels
and lift them up.
I do not witness the ordeal
of drying and changing clothes.
Even I struggle to extract
myself from my wet bathing suit.
But I almost feel ashamed
to be ambulatory, to be able
to walk with relative ease
across the wet tiles and back
into my life, unimpeded
by curbs or narrow doorways
or stairs, and I feel unworthy
to share in their physical therapy.

Blue Moon in July

It's a gray January afternoon
and I'm visiting my friend
in the nursing home. She has
a new calendar for the coming year
which another friend has annotated
with birthdays and other events
to help her remember. She's lost track
of minute to minute, let alone
day to day, and keeps asking
who brought the cookies? I did,
and patiently remind her again
and again. Paging through the months
she notes each full moon, and when
she comes to July, she cites two of them.
Let me see, I say, and note that July
will have two full moons this year.
The second one, I tell her, is a blue moon,
so called because they're rare.
She dutifully writes "blue moon"
beneath the circle in the square
for July 31, then continues tracking
full moons to the end of the year.

Now half the calendar is torn away
and the days are as long and hot
and bright as January's were brief, chill,
and drab, and the blue moon,
that metaphor for a rare occurrence,
is about to bloom on the horizon.
I imagine my friend finding
those words penciled on the last day
of July and hope she remembers
why she wrote them there.

Senior Prom at the Nursing Home

Every month there's a special event
for friends and family of residents
at the nursing home. This month
it's "senior prom" in more ways than one.
After a bland meal accompanied
by Frank Sinatra and Tony Bennett songs,
a hipster DJ commences to play
rap and hip-hop and other new sounds
to which these oldsters can't dance,
but some still try. Rising from walkers
and wheelchairs, they hold tight
to their partners to stay upright
while swaying or shaking vaguely
to the beat, barely moving their feet.
One gray-haired gal in a pink jacket
dances to every number, with or without
a partner, while the staff and the waiters
are the only ones who know the steps
and the music. A well-traveled couple
is crowned the king and queen
of the prom and handed the microphone
so they can sing an off-color song,
"Raised on gin, black as sin,
we're the team that always wins,
Nairobi!" while the black waiters
and nurses' aides, ignoring all
but the music, dance on, filled with grace.

All She Wants to do is Dance

I want to dance
somewhere with space
enough to writhe
to twist and wriggle
twirl and leap
so I venture out
in the dark to seek
a nightclub with a band
and find at first
a tiny bar, a jazz trio
tootling and whining
to no particular rhythm
where I'm crowded
by a quintet of detectives
also on the hunt
for something elusive.
I segue to the train depot
and raucous rock and roll
with an underlying thrum
like wheels on the rail.
I proceed to strut and whirl
becoming a blinding blur
in my fluorescent bodysuit
neon chartreuse or fuchsia
when the detectives
with their sportcoats and ties
mustaches and brush-cuts
grab me around the waist
hoist me above their heads
where I am suspended
on their upraised palms
until I slither down
and make a graceful bow.
In this scenario
I resemble Grace Jones
while the detectives all
look my father.
Did I commit the crime
they seek to solve
or are they supporting me

as I affront the patriarchy?
But this speculation
is too pretentious.
All I really want
is to dance, unpartnered,
with wild abandon.

Someone Should be Named Carlos

Carlos is missing from my life.
The young man next door
acquired a pitbull puppy—
brown and tan and handsome—
could this be Carlos?
He looked like a Carlos to me,
but I learned his name was Horace.
Horace? The Roman poet?
Horace Greeley? Horace Mann?
Go west, young man, and enjoy
your summer vacation from public school.
Emily Dickinson's dog was named Carlo—
close, but no cigar. Surely the proprietor
of Verde Seasons Lawns would be Carlos—
but no, he's Francisco. Do I even know
a Carl? Carl Jung, Karl Marx?
My grandfather's given name was Carl,
but he said that was the devil's name
and had his legally changed to Charles.
Who was his devil? His father?
Someone back in Germany whence
he emigrated in the 19th century?
But Carl is not Carlos. Carlos evokes
a kind of thrill, a dance, the clicking
of castanets, a beach of black sand,
and Carlos taking my hand,
luring me into the dangerous surf.

Inventing the Blues

My Choctaw friends tell me
that they invented the Blues.
"Call and response," they say.
That may be, but I think
it's as old as the echoing hills,
too ancient to ascribe to any tribe.
And the Blues is so much more
than that. There's the ululating cry
with no response. The primal wail
that gets you in your gut. And who
invented the guitar?
And what about the metaphors?
"Babe, I love your peaches;
let me shake your tree."
Those ripe and juicy peaches
have their own complex heredity.
You'd have to dig deep
to unearth the twisted roots
of that family tree.
When the Blues wash over me
I'm engulfed in a tsunami
of sound and feeling. I may be sad
but I'm glad to be alive
to ride that wild blue wave.

Thanks for the Blues

I started out with nothing
and still have ninety percent
of that left, and I know
I can't lose what I never had.
I also know I don't need
a weatherman telling me
which way the wind blows.
For all these gifts
I wrote a letter to the world
but had the wrong address,
used the wrong salutation,
don't even know
her real name.
I wanted to say thank you
for all the messages,
instant and delayed,
for filling me with awe
and sometimes terror,
for putting me in my place.
Thanks even for tornadoes
but also for rainbows
and a multitude
of nuanced hues,
but most especially
thank you for the Blues.

Vintage Years

I have wasted my life.
What was I thinking?
I have squandered my virtues
on unworthy persons.
Now all of life's seminal events,
except for the last, are in the past.
Nothing else awaits me—no new career,
no final love affair. It's the glass
more than half empty, almost drained
to the last drop. On the other hand,
it's a goblet that once brimmed
with an expectant bouquet that promised
this excellent vintage, the color of yet
a few more sunsets. Let me sip
the dregs and slowly savor every taste.

Bird Magic

Some days I imagine
that I could summon
a bird just by thinking.
For weeks I was taunted
by the calls of Flickers
but never saw one.
With that thought in mind
I sensed a sudden
movement in the hackberry
and there was a Flicker
hugging the trunk.
While I was working
at my desk, I recalled
that almost every fall
I've seen a Winter Wren
but not this year
when that little brown bird
suddenly appeared
outside the window
atop the denuded crape myrtle.
Of course, such expectations
must lie within reason.
This seeming magic
can never conjure
an out of place
Vermillion Flycatcher
or Cedar Waxwings
in the wrong season.
If wishes were birds
we'd all have wings.

Onomatopoeia

We fly backwards
to the primeval names of birds
hearing in the modern words
the primordial calls
of duck, duck, goose,
crow, crow, jay,
ancient onomatopoeia
echoing through millennia
and still today
the Pewee, the Phoebe,
the Dickcissel
call out their names
to the constant sky.

Natural Selection

I have no idols,
no paragons of perfection
to envy or emulate.
I don't look up
to anyone or anything
except perhaps the sky,
the tops of trees,
the Mississippi kite
in its season and others
too far aloft to name.
I only look down upon
the tiny blue bloom
nestled in the grass, the parade
of ants, a hovering bee.
We should accept ourselves
the way we are, the way
the bear accepts its fur.
Why should we aspire
to unnatural perfection,
when we've evolved
through centuries
of natural selection?

Images of God

If there is a god
the creatures made in god's image
are likely cats.
Consider the ocelot, the leopard,
the exquisite symmetry of tigers
or the whimsical asymmetry
of the calico cat
still with perfectly matched
green eyes and gray whiskers.
But also consider feathers and wings
and speed and flight,
scales and fins and gills
and the skill
to breathe under water.
So many creatures
are more beautiful and gifted
than human beings.
And we ourselves
are more and more mongrels,
perhaps have more in common
with dogs than with cats
with our slavish loyalty
to unworthy masters,
our eagerness to please
and learn new tricks
so we might be rewarded
with the occasional treat:
a job, a spouse, a raise,
a house, or heaven.

Hunting Happiness

E.O. Wilson said
that children are
by nature hunters
conjuring an image
of a small boy
armed with a BB gun
trying to knock
a blue jay off a branch,
but that's not
what he meant.
He was thinking
of his own childhood
quest for ants
rifling through grasses
to find that tiny species
and marvel at their industry.
As a child I too
was a hunter,
first of rocks,
hoping to discover
some crystalline
magnificence
hidden within,
then of fossils,
prehistoric
sharks' teeth,
the implant of a leaf
on a shard of shale,
and later seashells,
Scotch bonnets
and wentletraps,
intricate whorls
of limpets and snails,
and finally birds
that I still pursue,
my happiest moments
combing a beach
or scouring the crowns
of trees for the flutter
of wings, the tell-tale

flash of brightness,,
always hunting happiness
that rapt absorption
of seeking and finding,
a child forever.

Count on the Birds

I can count
on the birds.
Despite the vagaries
of the weather,
the moon, the stars,
and the calendar
say that it's spring
and the birds
of the season return
bearing bright feathers
to mark the pages
of the book
of lengthening days.

Spring Awake

Falling asleep with the promise
of rain in my mind,
I expect to be awakened
by thunder and lightning
but it's the mockingbird
that penetrates my dreams
of the cats escaping
and losing my way
in a barren moonscape.
He sings so convincingly
that I'm certain
dawn is imminent.
I stumble through the house
turning on lights, flip the switch
on the coffee maker, look at last
at the clock and discover
it's only 4 a.m. I deserve
two more hours of slumber,
so I turn off the lights,
climb back in bed and dream
of oversleeping and missing
a life-changing appointment
and awaken once again
to a new spring morning.

Birthday Poem –2023

The spring so far
has seemed to take
one step forward
and two steps back
every other day.
Today is my birthday
and I too am stumbling
forward toward
another decade
but fearful of losing
my footing.
It's Thursday,
Thor's Day,
filled with storms
and lightning and rumbles
of thunder. The blossoms
of the ornamental cherry
flutter down like snowflakes
while Dark-eyed Juncos
and wintering sparrows
are still on the ground.
But the Fish Crows
are back in town
hailing me
with taunting cheers
like midway barkers
at an amusement park
and the flowers
of the crabapple
are the candles
on my cake.

Rite

Tonight I go to steal
the irises from my neighbor's yard.
I have watched and waited
for the auspicious moment:
each day as I drive
home from work I glimpse
their green march up the hill
behind his house, the coming
of the buds, the first blue
blooms—perfect "fleurs de lis. "
They wait for me now, dark
on dark, almost scentless
except to the bee who ventures
deep inside the furred petals.
They tremble in the wind,
and if I do not save them now
tomorrow's storm will beat them down.
Tonight the moon will be full
to see by, the grass wet,
my scissor gleaming like Excalibur.
I'll cut the tall stalks
close to the ground, choosing
the half-opened buds to uncurl
slowly in the earthenware jug
on the hearth—cool blaze of blue tongues.

April For English Majors

The time-worn adages
seem not to apply
as the Earth copes
with the whims of weather.
One poet's contention
that this is the cruelest
month seems more apt
than another's quip
that April brings
showers sweet.
There's much wringing
of leaf and bud
from dry roots and stems
and much mingling
of remembrance and yearning
as we wait for the first
lilacs' blooming
while being delighted
by the artless singing
of an invisible bird.

Dark Eyes

I don't know
when they left
they didn't say goodbye
they'd just begun
to sing their songs
then silence
then others thronged
to fill the void
a trilling warbling
presence as evanescent
as the glancing spring
before summer
settled in
and I must await
autumn's return
to welcome them again

When Weather Threatens

When the weather threatens
don't run the vacuum cleaner—
it creates a vortex
causing the trees
to defy gravity
bending their topmost limbs
to touch the ground.
Don't wash the dishes.
Don't wash your face.
Don't answer the phone
or make a call.
Don't watch tornado TV—
those maps and live video
can't tell the story
of you huddled in the closet
as the mundane vanishes.

When the weather threatens
the gods return.
Zeus, Thor, Xolotl
are rearranging
the furniture,
changing blue to green
or painting the walls with rain,
spangling black ones
with splashes of lightning
and emptying
their ice chests at random,
blowing their shofars,
letting the Sirens,
Valkyries, Banshees
wail at will
from every direction
as all heaven lets loose
and the Earth seems to shake
while you, trembling in the dark,
suddenly see
that the invention of monotheism
was a big mistake.

Still Time

There will be time
I keep saying to myself
as I watch the weeds
creep up among the flagstones
of the patio and wayward
tufts of grass scattered
among the leaves of irises
pointing skyward in the flowerbed.
There will be time
to pull out wild onions
and the straw-like stalks
of last year's perennials,
time to stem the insidious sprawl
of day lilies and monkey grass
I swear I never planted.
But my hands grip themselves
rather than gardening tools.
The hoe and shovel hang
from the garage walls
along with rake and pruning shears
and my hands mimic the claw
that nestles with the trowel
in the bowl beneath the patio table.
I can no longer kneel
or reach and grasp to pull
the unwanted or gently tend
the plants I want to nourish.
There will be time, I say,
but now it seems there's only time
for the wild and unplanned to flourish
while my own time is nearing
the end of its growing season.

August Sonata

Cicadas and crickets
and other night singers
harmonize with the hum
of the air conditioner
while the air is as warm
as bath water
and the moon
is almost full.
Noise, heat,
moonlight seep
beneath the blinds,
creep around the windows,
keep me from sleep.
August is "august"
in terms of Celsius
and Fahrenheit
but some humbler month
would make for better nights.

The Chinese Written Character as a Medium for Poetry

In the fleeting dusk
of late summer
the sky above the yard
filled with Common Nighthawks
flapping and floating
and finally disappearing
in an eastward direction
to be replaced by a cumulus cloud
that at first revealed
the haughty profile of Ezra Pound
then quickly dissolved
as it too drifted to the east
trailed by a twittering drift
of Chimney Swifts
like the black strokes
of Chinese written characters
on the fading page of the sky.

Blue Butterflies

in memory of Barbara Momaday

At a friend's memorial service
I remember a Kiowa elder
intoning again and again
"That's the way I remember it,"
adding with each repetition
another long ago lost
family member to his list
but he never found words
for my lovely friend
whose death the event
was meant to commemorate.
Perhaps he simply forgot
as elders sometimes do
but I have not forgotten
that bright September day
in sight of Rainy Mountain
and still cherish the blue butterfly
I received as a memento
of the flight of that singular soul.

Blue Moon in October

I cannot say whether
this Blue Moon in October
bodes well or ill,
only that it's rare,
as rare and strange
as the sheaves of ice
that felled tree limbs
and snapped power lines
in this mercurial month
when we might expect
a brief Indian summer.
Those colorful leaves
still clinging to branches
became a glittering menace:
crystalline chandeliers
crashing from ceilings
the crack of gunshot
puncturing the morning,
and everything falling
and falling and the falling
of dark so complete
that the Blue Moon
has no other light
with which to compete.

Leaf-bird

The leaves caught up
in the November breeze
fly with such purpose
that I think they are birds
while the birds alighting
on bare-limbed trees
are so silent and dark
that I think they are leaves.

Emotional Content

Lately my daily horoscope
seems more like a poetry prompt
than a useful suggestion
or prediction. Today, for example,
I'm told that the conjunction
of Scorpio's moon with Uranus
will cause a possession
to "bring up surprising
emotional content."
I presume this means
some object in my home.
Marie Kondo's advice
never worked for me.
I find joy in even
the least of my possessions—
a sauce pan, a stone,
a pen—not to mention
paintings and books,
little boxes and figurines—
all are treasures,
all emotionally charged.
Where should I begin,
where to start the search
for today's evocative object,
and if I find the right one,
can I decipher its message?

Final Notice

A friend has died.
Since Christmas I'd expected
his usual phone call
thanking me for my letter,
wanting to know my plans
for New Year's Eve,
but the call I received
was from his nephew
saying, "We've lost him."

He was a long-time friend
but a bad influence,
sometimes a supporter,
then a betrayer, shifting
roles through decades
as we both moved
from place to place
and through the phases
of our lives, always seeking
something—was it love?
Recognition? A true home?

I imagine he'd be pleased
with his obituary
that omits all the rough patches
as it should.
I've already written
my own final notice
with similar omissions.
There's no need to list
life's vicissitudes.
Despite the ruts in the road,
the end is always the same.

Fading Fast

Thirty years ago
I was a Sugar Maple
in autumn,
hair aflame,
swirled in brightness,
long print skirts,
high-heeled boots,
dangling earrings,
standing out
even in the dark.

Now I'm any tree
in a wintry wood,
frosted over,
camouflaged
in denim and wool,
shod in hiking shoes
so I can navigate
this darkening
narrowing path.
I seem to be fading
more than aging,
and imagine my eventual
evanescence into a wraith,
a mere ghost
of my former self.

The Architecture of My Dreams

The pink Victorian house of my youthful dreams
with its hidden chambers and secret gardens
has been replaced in my eighth decade
by a vast complex designed by M.C. Escher
full of staircases and doors and elevators
that lead nowhere.
Some nights it's a university hall
where I wander meandering corridors
searching for the classroom
where my students await the final exam.
Other nights it seems to be an upscale hotel
whose winding stairs I scale
only to discover that I've lost the key
to my room and can't locate the reception desk.
Do I want to check in or check out?
Or it might be a sprawling hospital
where I follow the red line leading
to the emergency room, my heart thumping
an irregular rhythm in my aching chest,
when the red line turns blue
and a wrought-iron gate blocks
the longed-for entrance.
Still I always manage to excape
these labyrinths and dead-ends
and find myself standing at last
on a vast green lawn, wondering where
I parked the car, but when I awaken I know
it's safe in the garage of my one story home.

The End of the Year

I'd like to sit outside
and think about god
or maybe just watch
for a bird or two
or contemplate
the wrong turns
I've made in life
and even in my sleep.
Again and again I dream
of turning a corner
into an unfamiliar lane
and can't remember
where I parked my car.
I awaken with a start,
still lost. Now it's cold
and the day is darkening,
the feeders and sky are empty
of both birds and god,
and it's far too late
to turn back, to find
my way and start anew
as the year is dwindling
and an end inevitable.

How the World Ends

My father thought the world
would end in ice. His nightmares
featured stealthy glaciers creeping
close and looming large
at the edges of his sleep.

Mother dreamed the ocean's tides
crept farther and farther inland
but she could swim, perhaps forever
across a world awash.

But I know that the end
will be a slow fire burning
upward from deep beneath the earth
and then erupting in a conflagration
of our all-consuming and conflicting passions.

Blankets
after the blizzard

The yard and garden sleep
beneath a heavy blanket of snow
while I lie beneath white wool
and quilted coverlet emblazoned
with flowers that might grow
in a dream garden unknown
to a slumbering earth.
I dream there's a bear
tearing down the door
of the screened-in porch—
a porch from memory
attached to my childhood home.
Mother assures me
all will be well.
The door to the warm kitchen
is solid wood and locked
tight against the bear's approach.
As I struggle to awaken
I find myself trying to recall
Revolutionary and Civil War
battlefields I visited as a child,
sifting through names,
Gettysburg, Antietam,
finally settling on Yorktown
and a memory of Baked Alaska,
ice cream still frozen beneath
blankets of white meringue
and dark chocolate cake,
perhaps an apt metaphor
for the way the world seems
in this frigid dawn,
dark earth hidden
beneath a blanket
of wind-whipped snow
with a heart of ice
rather than fire.

Jennifer Kidney was born in Clarksburg, West Virginia, and grew up in Arlington, Virginia. She has a B.A. with Highest Honors in English from Oberlin College and a M.Phil. and Ph.D. in English Language and Literature from Yale University. She has been a babysitter, a Sunday school teacher, a cashier and concessionist at a movie theatre, a receptionist, a secretary, a university professor, a technical writer, and the director of nonprofit arts and humanities organizations and projects. She has won awards for her poetry, technical writing, service to libraries, teaching, brownie baking, and birding. She lives in Norman, Oklahoma, with her cats, Marvin Gaye and Priscilla Presley, and her Shetland sheepdog, Barry White. *This is the Truth* is her ninth book of poetry.

www.Ingramcontent.com/pod product-compliance
Lightning Source LLC
Chambersburg PA
CBHW011230120626
46549CB00008B/3221